From Beginning to End

A.E. Page

From Beginning to End

Contents

From Beginning
to End

Foreword

Love, a tale of two halves: the good and the bad, the happy and the sad, the light and the dark, the first and the last. *From Beginning to End* presents forty poems, exploring the many forms and faces of romance and relationships, including: the times that we loved; and the times that we lost.

To Mum, Dad, Lauren, and family and friends, this book is dedicated to you.

A.E. Page

In ascension: love above the cosmos.

I.
The Beginning

Answers

Do you know the questions to a secret, hidden world?
Can you understand that which should not be told?

Do you know the stories and songs of a secret, hidden home?
Can you understand that which is not yet known?

Do you know the passages to a secret, hidden land?
Can you understand that which is close at hand?

Do you know the answers of a secret, hidden whole?
Then I will protect you, heart and soul.

Whisper on the Wind

Whisper on the wind, will you, please.
Let the words fall into the ears,
like the leaves upon the trees.
Speak your mind, and let the pictures unfold.
Hear the inner warmth,
feel the outer cold.

Whisper the thoughts of a friend embraced.
See the person form, not to have seen a face.
Hidden from the eyes: those which judge the shell,
look to each word, and see
that there is more to tell.

In the ceasing warmth of sundown,
with feelings akin, is how it all started:
a whisper on the wind.

For You

As morning sun dawns and dust suspends in space,
light breaks in and shines on your face.
Though, to no surprise, you continue to sleep,
not opening an eye for one single peep.

I could not have asked for another,
no one else could ever do.
There is a first time for everything, though,
to believe it now seems untrue.

You give me the life of a fairy tale,
my treasure at the end of a quest.
Just to see your smile is sure worth the while,
and all of the things that you do best.

The people we are,
how we have come so far,
I will be right with you till the end,
and though at times we may hide,
I will be right by your side, and
I will always be your friend.

Best Friend

Your heart, I hear it,
your voice, I adhere it,
as we nuzzle to the comfort
of friendship.

Blanket Day

Chilly bodies run
afront fire's warmth and crackles:
blanket day for two.

Graffiti Love

Concrete jungle,
endless city sprawl,
lights along the boulevard,
graffiti on the wall.

Side street alleys:
veins of the city,
sounds of life,
night, so pretty.

Never-ending corners
of never-ending streets,
people all around,
stalls scented sweet.

Howling wind tunnels
sweeping through the trees,
new beginnings in the air,
floating on a breeze.

Art's seasoned parks,
ripples on a lake,
wispy clouds above:

a final great escape.

Moonlight shining down,
the sky a sultry blue,
I knock upon a door,
look up and see you.

With Love

Love is a friend,
old and new,
vacant from hate,
eminent from the start.

Love is a drug:
obsessive,
venturesome,
electric to the heart.

Love is patient,
omniscient,
versatile,
earnest in ardour.

Love is determined,
organised,
venerable,
embraced in valour.

Love is like magic:
occult,
vivacious,

enchanting until the end.

Love is like life:
original,
vital,
eloquent in trend.

Love is written in the stars,
ornate upon the pages,
veined throughout the future and past,
ensouled within the ages.

Love is to a friend so fair,
open pure and true.
Vale until the next we share,
ending, *With love* to you.

Wild Ones

When we were young,
when *we* were the wild ones,
we climbed the highest peaks,
stormed the widest lakes.
Nothing could stand in our way
when we were the wild ones.

We had it all, the world in our hands,
crossing horizons never-ending,
exploring kingdoms so grand.
We would dance under the dimming sun,
then lay and wait out for the stars to come,
when we were young, when
we were the wild ones.

And when we are old,
when *we* are the mild ones,
we will sit by and do as we please,
watch the clouds float by upon the breeze,
until our ship sets sail, as the leaves fall from their trees,
when we are old, when
we are the mild ones.

We have seen highs and lows,

good times and bad, still, many journeys await,

carving our path, so no matter what time,

no matter what may come,

a promise is a promise, no matter how young:

a promise is a promise, when

we were the wild ones.

Breathing Dreams Like Air

Breathing dreams like air,
so free, so fair,
in the midst of the moon sea glow.

Show of great display,
Celeste, cast away
to only a place we know.

Desire, design a fate so fine,
reward a smile awaiting time
and cross over the wavering shapes.

Imagine to be
a reverie, of love and life
in hallowed escape.

A Message

To write is a way of life, a way of love,
in all that has inspired so much.
To know all is never enough,
to share such care with simplicity's touch.

Indeed, go and seek meaning out,
for you may know what I am talking about.
Strike a word and you will not run amiss,
of a prelude's secret to knowing bliss.

Now in these words, I hear openness through,
of times to look most forward to.
For shame, the night strides ever on.
Where, oh where has it even gone?

For I know not, as with interaction,
time has waved farewell in splendid distraction.
Henceforth, it is time to rest,
with a well-earned sleep to give the best.

So listen to the story that has come to speak
in the ever latened week,
of a tale that has come to weave

such heavy eyes to take their leave.

To the wake of the morning,
and the day of dawning,
bid a fond good night,
in the closure of the breaking light.

Now morn arises with a knock at the door:
a familiar face back for more,
at wear with a smile to tell the ears,
at relish in moments of seconds to years.

So come once more, and reveal the secret,
for no matter what is done to keep it,
I will hear and blush red to the rose,
all in flush from head to toes.

Gleeful in joy and a simple youth,
that will last a face past knowing truth,
in this moment of feelings within,
at one with such a beaming grin.

To feel at one in warmth and care,
akin to that one comes to wear.
If only a message could take the hand,
and speak in air to understand.

Though care sees no end for two,
through each season and its cue,
so take the hand across the miles
and bring forth time to save the while.

To write is a way to show, a way to see,
in all that does start so small,
to know fondness found across distant ground, to be
a message to start it all.

Trains, Cranes, and Yellow Lined Lanes

Trains, cranes, and yellow lined lanes,
there as the station calls.
First time, a meeting, second time, again.
Trains, cranes, and yellow lined lanes,
romancing adventure out in the rain.
Down, down, down, curiosity falls.
Trains, cranes, and yellow lined lanes,
there as the station calls.

Waltz for Two

A time ago, youth and sprite came to meet
in rhythmical merriment and shimmering movement,
by the light of candles, to an ivory tune flowing,
winding the rivers of chance amongst a colourful sea
of bodies, twirling and swirling, as droplets embraced
the ocean's rippling form.

Two people, two opposites,
two strangers of face,
two pairs of feet
came to dance.

For All Time

Two children, explorers of life,
unaware of growing up,
sail the seas of imagination, on the ship of friends:
two rascals in a castle of dreams,
through whose eyes, nothing is as it seems,
run through the cornfields until the slumbering sun,
chanting "Best times, best times,
for all time, for all time".

Two adolescents, passengers of age,
learn the lessons of being human,
surviving the wilds of school, day and season after another:
two partners, now each with their own tears and laughs,
yet remaining together on a familiar path,
return to the cornfields of a childhood's past,
chanting "Best times, best times,
for all time, for all time".

Two grown-ups, companions of time,
search for new adventures,
ageing together, with wise minds and fanciful whims:
two people at mind with one another,
always a friend, a home, a keeper, a lover,

remain in the cornfields until the last stalk is gone,
chanting "Best times, best times,
for all time, for all time".

And if life were like a country song
that could be sung throughout the night time long,
dancing true to memory's tune,
right until the harvest moon,
chanting "Best times, best times,
for all time, for all time".

May Flower

Alike May flowers on a tranquil breeze, chilling spines till the
being stutters,

there you came, bequeathed in beauty, so striking, intricate,
aflutter,

turning day into night as the seasons passed by, until the
flowers bloomed,

riffling pages so quick, leaving covers untouched, to a feeling
internally doomed.

Alas, having left my sight so soon and sudden, was one not
to have known a name?

Where, now, this passion continues its search, that we might
meet again.

Remember Me

I stand on a hill
as light pierces the clouds,
a young warrior, naïve and proud,
gazing out upon the kingdoms:
the far reaches that we stem,
yet we can only go so far,
for we are just men.

Yet there is no end
to the kindness of love,
from which I have found
from my angel above:
an angel, my dearest,
from another realm,
striking my heart,
taking my helm.

Romancing the stone, you made me better,
older, wiser, with each passing letter,
and I can only see your kindness:
no fear, no hate.
I am humbled by your presence.
My future awaits.

Let me go, set me free,
but do not forget.
Remember me.

I awaken, in a room, cold and dark,
but in the corner, I hear
the beat of a heart:
a sound familiar,
a sound of times old.
I know you are there
in body and soul.

My angel, my queen,
all that is, all that has been,
to stop and think, and remember it so,
in the fields of gold,
your resonant glow.

We conceived worlds of our own,
did what we desired, as we sailed the star oceans
on the whims that transpired.
Though we are only human,
from the king to the queen.
Time catches us all, for we
are not machine.

As I run towards the settling calm,
searching for breath,
right into your arms,
I see your eyes, a stream of tears.
But please, be still.
Live fair, my dear.

We have lived our lives
together as one,
but now comes the night:
goodbye, the sun.

Our final moment,
our final touch.
My time has come.
Farewell, my love.

Let me go, set me free,
but do not forget.
Remember me.

Blessed Valentine

Count the blessings of an old-fashioned romance,
and I will find myself richer in love.
Take these words true and tie my bonds eternal,
and they will still say what is never enough:
my sweetest song.

Step by step, the sky circles above, around and around:
a trip of heart to the stars in reach,
to the wake of tomorrow, wrapped in warmth unbound,
a secret to share and teach:
my picture perfect.

Lose yourself to the bloom of days,
coming to worlds without time,
with my love always,
my dearest
Valentine.

Secrets

Come, I have got a secret to tell you,
of a little something I wish to say.
After all of that time passing, who knew
that blissful smiles so wide would come one day?
In the moment of askance, hand in hand,
songs of the harp strings of a sweet heart tug:
music old romantics can understand,
embraced whole in the warm fire of a hug.
Adventures await us to find ahead,
of times spontaneous and unrehearsed.
Dreamy inceptions for those still in bed,
thankful past a word for you being the first.
Wave as the sea bows on the lasting line,
and set sail into the big, blue divine.

Distance

By the virtue of patience
and the toil of compassion,
waters were bridged, by
two strangers of heart.

Where the boundaries of earth could divide,
not even souls could halt,
as hands in blossom merged
for the future together.

At the altar of fate, and
the eyes of the world,
figments walked into the light
as two friends of heart.

First Date, Part I

Sitting in a restaurant, waiting for the girl,
whose charm encapsulates time around her,
like the scent of warm bread in the morning,
like the coming of spring after the cold bite of winter:
an idol of happiness.

Here she comes now, walking past the front window,
with modest bounds in her stride,
and the glowing sun on her skin.
My palms become clammy and pulses flutter as I see her,
as my mind seeps away like melted butter.

Reaching for the door, she approaches, and
I find myself thinking of how this came to be,
what a wonderland I have come to,
as she comes to the table and sits,
her eyes full of life, depth and mystery,
looking into mine.

So we talk,
sweet.

First Date, Part II

Walking to a restaurant to meet the boy,
sunshine streaming through the tree-laden street,
casting upon the front window to where he waits within,
patient as the oldest oak,
immovable as the highest mount.

Arriving at the door, I see him clearly as I did that first day:
gratuitous, kind,
crazy, twined.
Now, here we both are,
the first date:
mine, his,
ours.

Entering the room, he looks up my way,
like a friend I have known for a lifetime,
and as he smiles, my nerves wash away:
a once cascading waterfall breaking up into a gentle stream,
calm and relaxed in such a dream,
in joy to be in this moment.

I sit as his eyes widen with tales,
looking into mine.

So we talk,
bliss.

In descension: lost beneath the chaos.

II.

The End

A Schism That Separates the Heavens

So off you went, to fulfil what you eternally dreamt.
You gave me an invitation, but this seems all that it meant:
just words on paper, not spoken from the heart.
Now to the beginning, the point where I start.

You gave me your all, but left none of your sorrow,
so to hold onto memory until the next morrow.
Hark this call, and eternity will be written,
as brittle and delicate as the heart once bitten.

Not once alleged was the penetrable blade.
Harbour the knowledge of discord, and see true love made,
for that of long lost, cycling sixes and sevens,
until the day you may ask: *Is love but*
a schism that separates the heavens?

Dark Heart

To flavour death's kiss
upon my bleeding lips, prise:
tempt thorns to my heart.

Truth and Reconciliation

Too many times have I seen that look on your face,
alike to a commander and his fleet.
Do you really think your life will sink away without a trace,
with all of your lies and deceit?

How many more have been in this position?
I could guess quite a few.
This must be child's play to you: a sacred tradition.
Is anything your mouth speaks out even remotely true?

Am I really that much of a burden to bear?
Be honest with yourself, when did you ever care?
Did it make you feel a king?
Did it make you feel stronger?
One can dig a deeper hole,
but for how much longer?

Cursed Shadows

When the time came to stop your nonsense,
you let guilt claim and cloud your conscience,
and upon that moment sparks did fly,
all within a matter of time passing by.

So, you continued draining life like a leech,
though by now, all was too late and far out of reach.
But still you destroyed the things wanted most,
as it slipped by you in the way of a ghost.

For you, this chapter, this story, will not end.
Though, knowing you, you will soon get the trend.
As grace falls, forget about your past,
as for you, it can only get worse.
But in the end, I guess that is what you deserve most:
a real life curse.

Believe in the Dream

Poison the chalice and take a sip, to
blooden the red of those ruby lips. Come,
kiss me—ever misty—to see on through.
A reckoning of roses and thorns stun:
my empress, my temptress, under the sun.
Stroll upon paradise shores, into dream.
Too in love? Well, too bad, with all to mean.
Another sentence, another restart:
rulers without rule—her king and his queen.
Befriending mirrors till death do us part.

Sweet as Honey

Sweet as honey, thick and runny,
faults and all to the moon and back.
Bright and sunny, joy so funny,
foot the ladder—an endless track.

It is the end of honeymoons,
breathing dreams like air far too soon.
Truth awakens balance and care:
partners, partners, most true and fair.

Unknown

Sitting on clouds untold,
spontaneous and subtle,
giving a chance
to second.

A Silent Voice

How do I know how you feel,
and understand that
which I cannot hear talking?
A silent voice.

Adoration

Adoration
is not an illusion.
Like magic, every part of it
is real.

War Games, Part I

Seconds pass by like a lifetime.
"What is mine is yours, what is yours is mine",
says a drug and its addict,
falling on knees, simply to have it.

Stories of fable claim an act of treason,
with the flipping of tables for no given reason,
but when euphoria finally meets its love,
like a viral bug, it cannot seem to get enough.

Words were said, and promises spoken,
as easily as they were broken,
and a being howls out, like a grenade ready to blow,
not caring to wait, not waiting to know.

Should a heart ever feel so serious,
as to at all appear disturbed or delirious,
then a fiend waits inside, like a hate needing freeing,
acting as one is doing, watching as one is seeing.

In the day, and the night,
in front of closed doors, all may seem alright,
but a mind can wander, and say other things,

seeking to be together, as a love and its sting.

Unable to cope when life is not the same,
a heart stops, races, towards its own pain,
sealing itself inside of a stasis
of a million-and-one different faces.

Reminded of the past, and of it all,
obsession finds itself against a wall,
looking out, but not able to see
the other side of what could be.

Flashing lights,
bound hands.
Time forgets not
to understand.

War Games, Part II

Time is running out of breath,
dwindling until there is nothing left.
The walls are slowly closing in,
blotting the light, until darkness wins.

Forever shackled, and bound in chains
is the war and its game
with a monster, an obsessive, an offender, a beast,
who does nothing, takes all: its hunger, its feast.

To be scared and unprepared in the face of betrayal,
wears a skin ever pale,
only able to take so much, only able to shed so many tears,
before drowning away in an endless ocean of fears.

To be called a cheat and a liar in a life melancholic
is the devil playing with fire, like an alcoholic,
as the scars on a face and the blood on a wrist
scream for the help and the life that they miss.

At night, all alone,
shakes a terror as it comes home,
dropping a heart just to survive.

What is now dead, and what is alive?

In what may seem like days, only minutes have past,
seeking a first, and finding a last,
picking up courage, and stopping to stare,
for what may still be lurking there.

Ears listen out to the incoming ring,
with faith resting on naked strings,
until someone somewhere cuts the line,
and eyes shut to their dark, looking for time.

Flashing lights,
helping hands.
Time forgets not
to understand.

Danse Macabre

Rain falls on the home as it does its occupants,

slowly eroding,

staining

a hovel of a home,

a hive of neglect,

a pair of lifeless beings:

two lily-of-the-valleys nestled in a blanket of melancholy,

striking heart chords where it hurts most,

neither one admitting their wrongs,

locked inside their own minds,

fixated on themselves, but

far too weak to leave the other,

each one leaching off

of what remains of dead hope:

a solemn swansong,

a danse macabre.

Glass Heart

Broken-hearted, hopes departed,
chances thwarted, on the floor, discarded.
My love uncharted, my mind unguarded.
For all that started, need be cathartic.

So much to choose, so much to lose.
Seemingly, time only brews more sorrowful news,
and what ensues only chews and screws,
when you ruse what your heart pursues
and you are only met with a further bruise.

What is it with me that I cannot see
after "no", after "no", after "no"?
I only wish to be in a life most happy,
that I know, I know, I know.

To have a heart broken,
I do not wish,
and now I have spoken,
I must be fixed.

Silky Thief

Feet strut by on a quiet eve:
temerity on legs, reflecting in the still waters of the riverside,
under passing lamplight with shimmering eyes,
a verdant emerald, like the jewels of a passion,
an unobtainable treasure, with lips bathed in deep,
alluring red, like the calling card roses of a killer,
a feline fatale, with a figure to distract and class to mask,
like a fool playing hard to get:
a silky thief, gone with my heart
into the night.

Untitled

Undiscovered am I,

not once seen,

ticking over: a day, a week, a month, a year,

inside and out,

turning over the page to yet another blank page,

left without words, left without a title,

ending up always back to nothing,

dying for the day to be loved.

Snow Light

Falling around me is snow light,
settling quaint on the ground,
as I walk down this path tonight,
knowing things cannot be.

As I wait on the other side,
holding nerves till they break,
in the hope that friendship survived,
I know that time runs short.

So hear me, and my heart is yours,
come to, and see the light.
Hold onto life forevermore.
In moments, I am there.

In the utmost depths of our hearts,
you know where you will find,
in the face where far futures start,
the courage of us all.

So when our day does choose to come,
do grace my hand with yours,
together in snow light and sun,

and venture forth to dream.

Fool's Gold

Good night, sweet romance, under
the velvet touch of
scarlet orange, as the moon
falls on the sun's love.
Gold shimmers with no
light, out from the mines of a
foolish tomorrow.

Oh, Oldest Ocean

Oh, oldest ocean, where is it that you take them?
They who have no breath of sin.
They who are woven into time.
Beseech to me your message of aeons,
and ascend the depths.

Can you not tell me of your tales
as time passes by so wearily?
Each day I search, and each day I float
further and further away,
as the waves roll over my feet.
Where are you, my love?

Under the stars of night,
I look into the oscillating currents of blue
and see beauty and kindness taken.
The light in the storm
that guides my ship yonder vale,
blackens in the tears of time
to become no more.

With a love undone
and day long gone,

for the faithful and the bold,

we cry to a love's lost,

oh, oldest ocean.

Where the Sun Once Shone, Where the Moon Now Shines

Where the sun once shone, where the moon now shines,
throwing a shadow on this heart of mine.
Solace in the bask, silhouette in wait,
afront its image to reciprocate.
Parades do flitter, with all effort in,
passing audiences with no hand out,
turning wheels in motion set deep within:
a day with no night does scarcely without.
Etch deep in the shallows, one can amend,
diving in the bottomless, black pretend.
Resurface up to the hug of the day,
casting an honesty to haloed signs.
Coupled as one lives in only two ways,
gracing us to where the sun and moon shines.

Blue Eye Blues

Behind the tears are those big, blue eyes,

deep as the sea,

headstrong,

alone for as long as time can remember,

until one day, thoughts will come to realise

that someone is waiting for you,

somewhere out there

in the vastness of the ocean, waiting to be swum.

In one moment,

in one sentence,

all will change, for a feeling strange,

as life courses the blues.

Appendix

Poems

1. Answers: 13/10/2017, Couplet
2. Whisper on the Wind: 15/09/2014, Free verse
3. For You: 27/06/2014, Free verse
4. Best Friend: 28/06/2014, Naani
5. Blanket Day: 08/03/2019, Senryu
6. Graffiti Love: 24/06/2014, Free verse
7. *With Love*: 03/05/2014, Acrostic
8. Wild Ones: 02/07/2014, Free verse
9. Breathing Dreams Like Air: 15/03/2020, Free verse
10. A Message: 22/08/2019, Free verse
11. Trains, Cranes, and Yellow Lined Lanes: 20/03/2020, Triolet
12. Waltz for Two: 18/05/2017, Free verse
13. For All Time: 31/05/2017, Free verse
14. May Flower: 25/06/2014, Free verse
15. Remember Me: 23/06/2014, Free verse
16. Blessed Valentine: 12/02/2020, Free verse
17. Secrets: 18/07/2019, Shakespearean sonnet
18. Distance: 07/03/2019, Free verse
19. First Date, Part I: 13/05/2014, Free verse
20. First Date, Part II: 13/05/2014, Free verse
21. A Schism That Separates the Heavens: 07/11/2010, Free verse
22. Dark Heart: 03/07/2014, Senryu
23. Truth and Reconciliation: 28/04/2012, Free verse
24. Cursed Shadows: 27/03/2013, Free verse
25. Believe in the Dream: 23/03/2020, Dizain
26. Sweet as Honey: 22/03/2020, Rispetto*
27. Unknown: 20/03/2020, Naani
28. A Silent Voice: 21/03/2020, Naani
29. Adoration: 16/10/2017, Naani
30. War Games, Part I: 01/07/2014, Free verse

31. War Games, Part II: 01/07/2014, Free verse
32. Danse Macabre: 05/05/2015, Free verse
33. Glass Heart: 01/05/2015, Free verse
34. Silky Thief: 04/06/2017, Free verse
35. Untitled: 10/05/2015, Acrostic
36. Snow Light: 21/09/2016, Ballad
37. Fool's Gold: 06/10/2017, Seguidilla
38. Oh, Oldest Ocean: 10/05/2015, Free verse
39. Where the Sun Once Shone, Where the Moon Now Shines: 22/03/2020, Shakespearean sonnet*
40. Blue Eye Blues: 15/08/2016, Free verse

*Form variation: Rispetto "Sweet as Honey" does not follow stress patterns; Shakespearean sonnet "Where the Sun Once Shone, Where the Moon Now Shines" uses a A-A-B-B/C-D-C-D/E-E-F-G/F-G rhyme and not A-B-A-B/C-D-C-D/E-F-E-F/G-G.

Forms

- Acrostic: stanzas of any lines, any metre, and any rhyme. First letters of each line spell a word, or words, when read diagonally. Themes vary. From Greece.
- Ballad: stanzas of four lines, metre of 8-6-8-6, and A-B-A-C or A-B-C-B rhyme. Often, even-numbered syllables are stressed, and odd-numbered syllables are unstressed. Themes focus on storytelling. From Europe.
- Couplet: stanzas of two lines, any metre, and A-A rhyme. Themes vary.
- Dizain: one stanza of ten lines, metre of 10, and A-B-A-B-B-C-C-D-C-D rhyme. Themes vary. From France.
- Free verse: stanzas of any lines, any metre, and any rhyme. Themes vary.
- Naani: one stanza of four lines, total metre between 20–25, and any rhyme. Themes often focus on relationships and statements. From India.
- Rispetto: two stanzas of four lines, metre of 8, and A-B-A-B, C-C-D-D or A-B-A-B, A-B-C-C rhyme. Even-numbered syllables are stressed, and odd-numbered syllables are unstressed, and can be written as one stanza of eight lines, with a metre of 11. Themes vary. From Italy.
- Seguidilla: one stanza of seven lines, metre of 7-5-7-5-5-7-5, and A-B-C-B-D-E-D rhyme. Lines 4–5 have a pause in between, a tonal shift, and often, a stop. Themes vary. From Spain.
- Senryu: one stanza of three lines, metre of 5-7-5, and no rhyme. Themes often focus on human nature. From Japan.
- Shakespearean sonnet: one stanza of fourteen lines, any metre, and A-B-A-B/C-D-C-D/E-F-E-F/G-G

rhyme. Stanzas comprise of three quatrains and a couplet, metres remain consistent, and often, even-numbered syllables are stressed, and odd-numbered syllables are unstressed. Themes vary. From England.

- Triolet: one stanza of eight lines, any metre, and A-B-A-A-A-B-A-B rhyme. Line 1 is repeated in Lines 4 and 7, and Line 2 is repeated in Line 8. Themes vary. From France.

Printed in Great Britain
by Amazon